D1826512

Some Complicity:
Poems & Translations

Harry Thomas

Un-Gyve Press

Library of Congress Control Number:
2013943894

ISBN: 978-0-9829198-2-8

10 9 8 7 6 5 4 3 2 1

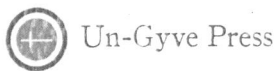 Un-Gyve Press

Designed by Un-Gyve Limited.

The title typeface is Bodoni, Giabattista Bodoni, and Garamond, designed after the original Claude Garamond types, is used for the text throughout.

Christopher Ricks is the Literary Advisor to Un-Gyve Press, an independent imprint of The Un-Gyve Limited Group.

Un-Gyve Press Boston
www.un-gyvepress.com

The Un-Gyve Limited Group
139A Charles Street, No. 393
Boston, Massachusetts 02114-3282 U.S.A.

For Adriana

I am worth more for your walking by.
My blood is redder for your loveliness.

After the Paiute

Contents

II. Translations from Italian

Acknowledgements

I am grateful to the editors of the journals in which these poems and translations first appeared:

The Alternative Review: "Many Are Called"

Cauldron: "Little Elegy"

The Formalist: "Elegy," "Mother, 1961," "Poem"

Harvard Review: "Pliny," "To Himself"

Los Angeles Review: "The Sunset at Fossoli"

Literary Imagination: "Al Anbar, Iraq," "At the Old Los Angeles Zoo," "Brown Battalion," "Deor," "Grandfather," "Heroism," "In the Smoke," "Late at Night," "Mt. Palomar," "Sorapis, 40 Years Ago," "The House of the Customs Men," "The Infinite," "The Little Girl of Pompeii," "To pass the noon"

Modern Poetry in Translation: "Singing," "Wooden Heart"

Poetry Nation: "The Snail"

Poetry Northwest: "The Goat"

Salamander: "Saturday in the Village," "The Thaw"

Sewanee Review: "Contagion"

Slate: "Of Country I Know," "Richard Noel"

Song: "The Text"

Southern Review: "Absence," "Mountain Meditation," "Poem," "Seasonal"

TriQuarterly: "Xenia I," "Xenia II"

Some Complicity:
Poems & Translations

I. Poems

Deor

Old English

Wayland in Värmland
suffered adversities,
that strong-minded man
knew misery.
Bitter setbacks, pains
of winter cold, these
were his companions.
His truck was with trouble
after Nithhad had done
the violence to him—
hacking his hamstrings,
hobbling the better man.
    —That was endured;
    so may this be.

Beadohilde despaired
when her brothers were butchered,
but when she was sure
she carried a child—
that was what wrecked her.
She couldn't conceive
of a future.
    —That was endured;
    so may this be.

We've all of us heard
how the Geat loved Mathilde,
loved her without limit,
loved with such love
his sleep was shattered.
    —That was endured;
    so may this be.

Thirty years Theodric
ruled the Maeringa's town.
The facts are all known.
      —That was endured;
      so may this be.

We all know of Eormanric
and his wolflike ways—
subjugating subjects
the length of Gottland.
He was a cruel king!
Men sat unmoving,
shackled to sorrow,
thinking just one thing—
to cut the king down.
      —That was endured;
      so may this be.

Of myself I'll say this:
I was once the poet
of the Heodingas,
dear to my lord.
My name was Deor.
Winter to winter
I had a good holding,
a lavishing lord.
Now one Heorrenda,
a masterly man,
finds praise in the place
until lately my lord
gave to me.
      —That was endured;
      so may this be.

Of Country I Know

for David Ferry

Above the lower tree-line in the desert
northeast of San Diego, where I'm from,
in land mapped out abruptly by the sun,
you'll find a spreading growth of piñon pine,
juniper, branching nearly to the ground,
lilac and sage, and scattering white pines.
Even in the driest months of summer
(in some years summer lasts through late November)
where there are seeds and insects there will be birds
and small, ground-dwelling, furtive creatures too.
Hummingbirds nest in the cactus scrub;
woodpeckers bore homes in the crazy yuccas;
meadowlarks shelter in the slender reeds;
lizards slip in and out of rock crevices,
panting and scurrying on the hot sands;
coyotes prowl all night for a square meal.

Everywhere life goes on against the odds.
You stand in the middle of a riverbed
the wind has driven down since there was wind
and like as not, three feet below the surface,
rimmed with a crust of alkaline deposits,
or where there's mesquite or a clump of bunch grass,
there's water left from last year's winter rains.

Mt. Palomar

for my brother Charlie

The tour had lasted nearly an hour already,
and what with the slow walk in the heat to the dome,
and the docents' recitations and dumb jokes,
the children in tow appeared eager to go home.

Though in the dome's dim light it was hard to tell.
And much of the time, I admit, I was all ears
to hear that mother's Corning made the great mirror—
made two, in fact, the first one a failure; that years

went by, George Ellery Hale growing frailer,
before the polishers in Cal Tech's shop
were finally done—the War deflecting them,
the Pyrex/silica disk covered up;

that the huge horseshoe tube that holds the mirror,
a million-pound precision instrument,
floats on a mere 3/1000 of an inch of oil,
the pressure of one hand enough to move it;

that the dome, bigger than the Pantheon,
rotates on tracks so smoothly no vibration's
transmitted to the telescope; that when
the telescope at last looked at the heavens

the photographs of spiral nebulae
proved once again the universe's expansion,
a theory even Einstein had disputed
until, in '31, he visited Mt. Wilson.

Then we were taken through an opened door
and told to stand along the metal catwalk
that runs around the dome, the sunlight blinding.
And as a docent started in to yak—

"That small dome there's the Oscar Mayer dome"—
I felt a movement under me. "Hold on,"
I said. And everyone looked wonderstruck,
and braced themselves for orbiting the sun.

At the Old Los Angeles Zoo

Inside the first enclosure,
Beside the picnic tables
The city has installed,
Amid the trash and trash barrels,
Where lions, bears, elephants
Or some other species
Roared growled blared clamored
Because of where they were,
As I was taking notes
And a tattooed young man
Was saying in the '60s
The city's citizens
Passed an initiative—
What in California
We call a proposition—
To close this place at last,
Where the animals were known
To be abused and even
During World War II
Had their food rationed,
Half of it being sent
To soldiers overseas,
And next to the hanging bag
Of toxic black drip—
The Rescue! Disposable
Yellow Jacket Trap—
The sign above me read,
"Do Not Feed the Wildlife/
Fine and 6 Months in Jail."

April 10, 2010

Going On

By the water tank
Near the top of the park
A long snake lay sunning
On the path I was taking.

It seemed nonvenomous,
Though a snake in the grass
(Whose bite I've felt)
Likewise lies inert.

But unlike that kind,
This basked in the sun,
Straight and harmless,
Letting me pass.

The Walk

As I walked out
To take the walk
I take most days
To work off lunch,
However meager,
And clear my head,
I met a man
Climbing the hill
That I go down.
"You can't see them,"
He said, his voice
The voice it seemed
Of disappointment
Or consternation.
"Sorry," I said,
Meaning, of course,
"What do you mean?"
Not "That's too bad."
He squinched his face
As to express
His puzzlement
At what I meant,
And went on up.

I knew at once
He wondered why
I was on foot
For any reason
That wasn't his.
It's not a city
In which one walks.
Then when I reached

Armada Terrace
And saw six men
Standing, looking,
Five of them through
Binoculars,
The other through
A telescope,
And all of them
At the same thing
At the North Island
Naval Air Station,
I stopped to see
If I could see
Between the houses
What they were seeing
Beyond the hill,
Across the water,
And thought I saw
Lines of small planes,
Metallic glints,
Among the standard
Fighters and bombers
And Quonset hangars
On the hectares
Of dun concrete.
And then I heard
Behind me, blaring
From a huge truck
Two men had parked
Any which way
Just up the street,
The radio—

A man announcing
The play-by-play
Of an air show.
I knew that voice.
It is the voice
Of pro football:
FIRST DOWN AND GOAL!
But then he said:
NOW THE MARINE
CORPS FIGHTER JET
(He screamed its name
Ecstatically)
ITS MISSILES LOCKED
READY TO RAIN DOWN
DEATH AND DESTRUCTION.

A lovely day.
No clouds at all.
The moon a faint
And sheenless disk
Against the blue—
Otherworldly.
On Owen and
San Fernando
The pepper trees
Lining both streets.
There's one I love
At the far end of
San Fernando,
Its trunk so massive
And with so many

Protuberances
Of such strange shapes
Arcimboldo
Might have dreamed it.
Along the shore
Beside the path
The small blue heron
And snowy egret
Tiptoe together
From stone to stone
And then go under
To feed on fish
Too small to see,
Except they see.

I missed them too.
For I went home,
Back up the hill
And up the stairs,
And in my room,
The door shut tight,
I sat and wept.

February 6, 2011

The Text

It says that in the bone marrow of a man
you can trace the outline of a boy's small bones.
Where, when seven, a knee knocked against gravel,
or the left cheek caught like cloth on a nail,
or an ankle snapped, twig-like, falling out of a tree,
the hurt is remembered, tissue and tale, in the bone.

Gelatinous things, such as slugs and snails and sea mollusks,
are different, and the same.
Unskeletal, indefinite on their own,
they live in a series of buffed hollow bones.
They leave us their stories like braille.

Think too of those boxes that fit inside one another
like layers of skin, tree bark, winter clothes.
Watch how the child lifts and puts aside the outer,
impatient for the core.

It takes a thick hidden thing to sustain us.
The mind comes and goes and then gives out like a quarter.
The gray grain in the bone is gold.

Admission

The turnstile *was* there to the left, then right,
Then straight ahead. I groped inside my pocket
For money for a ticket, but the Ticket
Booth suddenly was shuttered for the night.

I thought of Harrison and his H clocks,
The problem seemingly insoluble
Of sailing safely anywhere at all,
The seamen dreaming anxiously of docks.

Contagion

Sometimes when we wake day isn't day
but a dream that didn't unwind,
a stain we can't wash away.
We luff until noon, then surrender
days in a chain to that sway.

Hard work is a cure for some men.
For some nothing works. I try
taking a kayak upriver
or tracing the moon in its shadow,
but no matter what I do it stays.

It will stay until one week
ends in exhaustion, as in
a ramshackle house on whose walls
even the swearing has faded,
and our room is ready.

I lie still and listen.
Sure as the river, sure
as the moon that could not cleanse,
this insistent contagion inside me
goes on.

Poem

Tonight will be silence and snow.
Tomorrow at your window, looking out
at white, all white, will be
like lying down to sleep at nightfall,
the light in your eyes still lingering,
your eyelids the last leaves sinking.

Song

I want to be a shoe: a shoe
left under the bed after a bad life

or out under a bench in the cold
until the leather breaks.

To be a shoe with white laces,
white as chalk, white as bride's white.

A shoe of death, a baker's shoe
that rats will take for bread.

And I want to be a shoe like a bucket
to stand in, until I overflow.

Richard Noel

He said he'd be absent a week,
and when I asked him why,
he looked away from me.
A small boy, and very shy,

he never spoke in class,
except to tell us about
bees, say, or the Burgess Shale.
I couldn't figure him out.

Two or three minutes passed—
as much as I could stand.
Then: "There's a tumor on
my pituitary gland."

He hadn't slept well in years;
watched scientific shows.
The doctor to remove it
would enter up his nose.

To finish the long profile
his grade depended on,
the afternoon before
the surgery, alone,

he worked late in the library.
I saw him typing away.
On my desk were his ten pages
the first thing the next day.

Over the years I, too,
have had hard things to face.
But when did I once summon
such fortitude or grace?

Poem

This morning I said to myself
at night you will write a poem,
no matter how late it is
or how insipid the poem.
It was only a promise to save
something from a day
about to be given over
to work I had to do—
some token to set down
beside my glasses and watch
on the night table, dated
Thursday, July the 12th.

Al Anbar, Iraq

A car approached a checkpoint that Marines
had thrown up on the road that afternoon.
The car's brakes failed. The soldiers opened fire.
Somehow before the bullets struck, the woman
and the two children in the back got out.
The man was hit; killed instantly. Then. There.
But the man's wife was told he had survived.
(Who told her that? Or had she to believe?)
Some soldiers, a lieutenant and his men,
were ordered to correct the wife's mistake.
"We gave the woman money," he recalled,
"and gave her crates of water, maybe ten,
and gave the kids, like soccer balls and toys.
We didn't really know what else to do."

Many Are Called

i.m. Joseph Brodsky

"I think it is a gift from God," I read
Again, this sentence of the undefiled,
And wonder at it still. I see you now
As I first saw you: slumped against a wall,
Smoking, your right hand slipped inside your shirt,
Remote from us on your offending Elba.
That night, your bad heart working well, we beat
The cold back, talking, almost to the river,
Your gift imploding English as though you'd made it.
Later, we wondered. You foretold the last
Draft you'd make on God's gift: gone back to Russia,
Upright against the Crosses' wall you'd stand,
Close by St. Peter's domes, the lemon Neva,
Your right hand held gun-level at the guns
Of conquered Mongols, Georgians, Serbs,
To take your place in legend: "Pardon me, boys,
Is that the Chattanooga choo-choo?"

Absence

1

Last night I dreamed of Genji on the shore
at Suma, three years, huddled in his hut
beneath the torrents, exiled from her touch.
His cloak wrapped round him tightly, and his mind
dissolving in the memory of her flesh.
Waking and sleeping. No relief. In dreams
the wind from off the cliffs brings back her voice
and wet sleeves waving through descending leaves.
Then, near dawn, wading in the sea, alone,
he thinks that he can taste her in the spray.

2

And here, a dry wind pulses through damp trees,
and cars drift by my window with the sound
I think of, late at night, lying alone
in Ann Arbor; the sound of winter surf
below the cliff, booming against the rocks,
spraying our words. Now, at this distance, words
are letters, voices that our memories
can merely guess at, as, in the interval
of quiet, of no wind, cars, or surf, we move
together, with three thousand miles between us.

Seasonal

for Adriana

Three months of winter. Absence
is all here. Absence of sun-
light on the icy stream and
in the hickory branches
lined with snow. Absence of leaves:
the trees reduced to rigid
quadrants, geometric graphs.

A brutal, aimless absence,
where at evening I have seen
pairs of robins foraging
for the fermented sweetness
of wrinkled apples. They peck
and pivot above the fields
like sparks on the wintry air.
Yet, more than once, a sick male
has mistaken a window,
wavering with warmth, for an
open, unending passage,
angled against it, and died.

Three months of winter. Absence
of love, not less than sunlight,
fails me. And then, this evening,
a hint at return: a plane,
seemingly a moth, winged by
and, reflected in the cold
glass on the desk where I read,
silently entered my ear,
as though it would propel me
to some presence, maybe yours.

Poem

That morning when I saw you for the first time,
sitting in a classroom with light-blinded windows behind you,
and smiling the smile I have never tired of seeing you smile,
self-conscious as I was I stared at you
as though I would go on staring forever.
And suddenly I felt my mind whirling out of itself
and then that feathers were unfolding
from the middle of my back and shoulder blades
and I was being lifted into the air.
The room grew still, and I, beholding you,
wrote down these lines that I am writing now.

Night

In your now slow-footed way,
Made even slower by the dark
Of the middle of a winter night,
You appear at the side of the bed,
An apparition or dream figure
To me all at once wide awake,
And at your seeming incredulous
And seeming indignant "Yes"
To my asking if you're all right,
I understand my asking it
Was for my sake as well, because
It was just thirteen years ago
We spent a year in hospitals
To beat the cancer in your brain,
Doing whatever we could do
So that you might stand here tonight
Back from an aging woman's pee.

Impediment

To hear from just one ear
Is to hear half of all
There is to hear, or hear
It all, but half as clear.

Each seems a loss to you,
Though really, dear, it all
Depends on what or who
You have to listen to.

Mother

Out of the canyons came,
day after rainless day,

that summer we moved in
to the house on the canyon's rim,

tarantulas and scorpions
and five-foot rattlesnakes.

Older than my brothers,
I'd shout to keep away

and run to get our mother,
who'd run to get the rake.

The rattlesnakes were scary,
drawing back only to strike.

The scorpions were quick,
sideways as well as ahead.

The tarantulas, all hairy,
had bands a satanic red.

With four small sons beside her
she did what she had to do:

she slaughtered every spider,
split every snake in two.

She smote with greater force
following the divorce.

Mountain Meditation

We drive northward. The mountain corridor
darkens around the rims as clouds converge
and mask the light. On the slopes, sycamore
and oak surrender to the hills the rite
of casting shadow. Reticent as sleep,
and cool in this metal shade, my mother leans
beside me, struggling mildly to retain
her faith, and knowing I have none of it.
It has been so for years. And I look away,
where, turning up a sudden flue of light,
I see among the clouds confronting me
my pale blue spectre shining in the glass.

Little Elegy

I found you on the floor
holding out your hand,
palm up and open, as when
severe and professorial
you'd determined
to prove some point to a friend.
But the arrogance gone
you seemed hollow, a box
exposed at the end of the trick,
and the hand that I'd seen
for hours in the yard,
tamping, uprooting,
instructing the delicate
lilies to grow,
that hand was held like a beggar's,
like Jesus' suffering the children to come,
like anyone's at a window
checking for rain.

Grandfather

You weighed so little when I picked you up
from off the kitchen floor where you had died
that morning making coffee, the white cup
now shattered into pieces at your side,
and you—exposed through your white boxer's fly,
and took you to the back room to your bed
and laid you down and sat and waited. I—
I was sixteen. My first time with the dead.

I sat there on the bed as if to stay,
not going out to grandma and my brother
despite their desperate crying out for you.
I watched the palm fronds in the window sway
in the slow summer air...And then my mother,
then paramedics, came, and I withdrew.

On a Postcard from My Father

Today, the Spanish Steps—this 5 x 7
reductive roof shot, birds and beggars gone.
Even the air's been brushed above the booty
you're "worn out" taking on Via Condotti.

Meanwhile, I down stale coffee, flick an ash,
and resubmit to Kafka's senseless *Letter*,
index fingers cocked into my ears
against those choppers droning back to base.

The Loop

We were more and less than an estranged father and son.
Years went by like clouds in indifferent silence.
Would we even have known each other on the street,
At a corner, say, waiting for the light to change,
Or under the El in downtown Chicago?
We've flown in from our two ends of the continent
And both put up for the night at the Palmer House.
I'm just emerging from the revolving door
To walk over for an hour at the Art Institute.
The wind has blown your hat off down the street
Brim over crown, and I run after it.
When I hand it back you thank me for my kindness.

A Dream of Complicity

A stylishly dressed, beautiful, middle-aged, blonde woman, a woman I don't recognize, comes out of a hotel or upscale apartment building, probably in Los Angeles, though it's now 2008, not the '50s when we lived there, and raises her hand to flag down a big car—a Chrysler, it seems like—being driven by another middle-aged woman, this one with a shock of dark hair. (I am across the street, my vantage a cameraman's—perched high on a boom above the scene.) She walks up to the driver, who has stopped in the middle of the street, and hands her money, perhaps a lot of money, perhaps as much as $1,000, and then I hear her instruct her to drive by the building again, as many times as it takes, until she attracts the attention, driving slowly, looking his way, of my father sitting behind the darkened glass in the lobby of the hotel or upscale apartment building. The woman agrees to do this, nodding, and sure enough on her third time driving by, my father spots her and she knows she has caught his eye. She drives by once more, and as she comes near the hotel or apartment building my father pulls out from the building's underground garage in a white finned Cadillac. I breathe hard when I see him pull out because now I am sitting in the back seat of the Chrysler, my arms folded on the top of the leathery front seat. It runs in my head that he has told his wife—who it suddenly comes to me is my wife—that he has to go for a ride, has said it the way a husband says such a thing, the way Adam Sandler says it to Tea Leon in *Spanglish* after he has begun to fall in love with Paz Vega. "I have to get out," Sandler half whines, "have to get some air." But when my father says it it's a naked ruse for him to set out in the hope, say, of spotting the woman in the Chrysler. She and I follow my father in his white

Cadillac, but only for a few seconds, a hundred yards or so, when, to my surprise, just as the road bends downhill out of sight of the hotel or upscale apartment building, he pulls over and parks, gets out of his car, and walks to the passenger side of the Chrysler. He opens the door and gets in, looks at the woman, and says something to her that I don't quite hear, because now I am lying, naked, on the floor behind the front seat of the Chrysler, so that my father won't see me. He is asking her where she is from. "Eastern Europe?" My father wouldn't have known an Eastern European woman from a South American, a Hungarian from an Argentine. But he says very little to her, and she says nothing to him, but, I imagine, stares straight ahead, all business. He is feeling her out, though at the same time he is preening within, thinking, after all, that a woman driving by his building, seeing him dimly through darkened glass, has immediately taken a fancy to him and driven again and again by the building in order to arrange this meeting. After a while—I can't tell how long—it is night, far up the coast, Carmel, it may be, and the car comes to a stop in a small parking lot. My father gets out and walks toward the rear of the car. I am anxious that he will see me. Pressing myself lengthwise against the back of the front seat, I think to myself I ought to have told the woman to be sure to turn off the nightlight before she stopped so that when my father, who will be sure to walk to the rear of the car where he might, glancing down, see me, would, if glancing down, be looking into a dark car and so less likely to see me.

Elegy

After Catullus

Having driven two hundred miles through towns
of strangers, by cabins, trailers, Mormon outposts,
I have come, brother, to your mountain grave,
a month too late to do my part in the service,
and years too late to set things right between us.
What words are there after so long a silence—
the need to make a living took me from you,
and then the life you chose took you from me?
Let a few wildflowers and an old love be all,
brother, you have from me forever. Farewell.

II. Translations from Italian

To Himself
Giacomo Leopardi

Now, worn-out heart,
you'll rest for good, the last deception dead
that I believed was deathless. Dead.
I'm sure
not just the hope, but the desire
for sweet illusions is all gone.
So rest for good.
You've had enough excitement. Nothing's worth
all that you've suffered, nothing's good enough
on the whole earth.
This life is bitter, tedious,
and never any better. The world's shit.
So take your rest.
The one thing that's in store for us
is death. Show your contempt for it
and nature's brutal power that,
though hidden, governs everything—
the infinite vanity of everything.

The Infinite

Giacomo Leopardi

I've always loved this hill off by itself
and this hedge screening off so much of all
there is out there to the horizon line.
But sitting here now, gazing out again,
I'm filled with a new sense of boundless space
and more-than-human silences and stillness,
and for a while my heart is not alarmed.
And listening to the wind riffling the hedge
I find myself comparing it with that
infinite silence, and I think again
of the eternal, of seasons past
and the too-present present and its sound.
So in this immensity I drown.
And going under's easeful in this sea.

Saturday in the Village
Giacomo Leopardi

As the sun sets
the girl comes home from the country,
carrying a bundle of grass
and a handful of roses and violets.
With these, the custom is, she gets
ready for tomorrow, the holiday,
adorning her breast and hair.
On the steps with her neighbors
the old woman sits spinning, her face
to the disappearing day,
and tells the story of her good time
when she'd adorn herself
and, still slender and full of grace,
dance the night away with those
who were her friends when she was lovely.
Now the air darkens,
the sky turns blue, and shadows fall
already from hills and roofs
in the whitening new moon.
Now the bell gives a sign
of the holiday to come:
and at that sound you would say
the heart is comforted.
The swarm of children
in the little square, shouting
and leaping here and there,
makes a happy noise.
And meanwhile the gardener goes,
whistling, to his meager meal,
thinking ahead to his day of rest.

Then, when every other light is spent,
and everything else is silent,
you hear the rapping hammer, the saw
of the carpenter, who stays up
in his closed shop in the lamplight
and hurries, pushing himself
to finish his work before dawn.

Of the seven days this day
is the day for thanksgiving.
Tomorrow the hours will bring
boredom and sadness,
and everyone will return
to the thoughts of the usual labor.

Playful boy,
this flowering time
is like a day of joy,
a cloudless day that heralds
the holiday of your life.
Be glad, my little boy.
It's a sweet state, a happy season.
I won't say more—only
this holiday that is about to come
let it not be heavy for you.

The Goat
Umberto Saba

I've talked with a goat.
She was tethered
alone in a meadow.
Stuffed with grass, rain-
soaked, bleating.

That bleating going on and on
was the brother of my sorrow.
So I responded, first as a joke,
then because sorrow is eternal
and speaks in a voice that never varies.
I heard that voice
in the moaning of a solitary goat.

In a goat with a Semitic face
I heard a cry against every evil,
the crying of every life.

In Memory
Giuseppe Ungaretti

Mohammed Sceab
was his name

Descended from a line
of nomadic emirs
a suicide
because
he had no country

He loved France
and changed his name

He was Marcel
but not French
though he no longer knew
how to live
in a tent of his own
listening to the melody
of the Koran
sipping coffee

And he didn't know
how to free
the song
of his abandonment

I accompanied him
with the woman who ran the hotel
where we lived
in Paris
at number 5 rue des Carmes
dull downhill alley

He lies
in the cemetery in Ivry
a suburb
that always looks
like the day
when a fair
is dismantled

And it's possible
that only I
know that he lived

from *Ossi di seppia*
Eugenio Montale

To pass the noon, intent and pale,
beside a scorching orchard wall,
and hear in the dry thorny brake
clicking thrushes, a rustling snake.

On the cracked ground or in the vetch
to spy on the red ants in files
that now break up and now crisscross
the pinnacles of little piles.

To see through leaves the distantly
palpitating scaly sea
as all at once from the bald peaks
rise the cicadas' tremulous screaks.

And walking in the dazzling sun
to feel with sad amazement
how all we are and go through 's in
this following a wall up on

the top of which jagged bits of bottles run.

The House of the Customs Men
Eugenio Montale

You don't remember the house of the customs men
on the hillside above the cliff overhanging the reef.
Desolate, it has waited for you since the evening when
the swarm of your thoughts entered it
and paused, irresolute.

Southwest winds have lashed the old walls for years
and the sound of your laughter has lost its gaiety.
The compass for no reason at all goes crazy,
and the dice come up numbers no one guesses.
You don't remember; another time confuses
your memory; a thread is being lost.

I hold an end of it still; but the house
draws away and the smoke-blackened weathercock
on the rooftop whirls unpitying.
I'm holding an end; but you stay alone,
not breathing here in the dark.

Oh the fleeing horizon! where the light
of a tanker rarely flashes.
Is there a way through here? (The sea still crashes
against the crumbling cliff.)
You don't remember the house of this evening of mine.
And I don't know who goes and who remains.

Xenia I
Eugenio Montale

1

Dear little insect
whom we called Mosca—I don't know why—
this evening just before dark
as I was reading Deutero-Isaiah
you reappeared at my side,
but not having your glasses
you couldn't see me,
and without their glinting
I couldn't be sure
it was you in the dusk.

2

Without your glasses or antennae,
a poor insect who had wings
only in imagination,
a Bible coming unbound
and largely unreliable,
the black of night, a lightning flash,
a thunderclap, and then
no storm. Can it be
you were gone so quickly
without saying a word?
But it's ridiculous to think
you still had lips.

3

At the Saint James in Paris I'll have to ask
for a single room (they don't like
the odd guest). And also at your faux
Byzantium hotel in Venice;
and then immediately go down to find
the switchboard operators' cubbyhole—
those girls who were always your friends;
only to give up again—
the telephone connection lost—
the desire of having you back,
if only in one habit or gesture.

4

For the afterlife we had devised
a whistle, a sign of recognition.
I'm trying variations of it in the hope
we're all already dead without knowing it.

5

I've never understood
whether I was your dog,
faithful and sick with distemper,
or you were mine.
To others you were a myopic insect
at a loss in the blah-blah
of high society. They were naïve,
those clever ones. They didn't know
they were your laughingstock:
that even in the dark you made them out,
unmasking them
with that infallible sense of yours,
your bat radar.

6

It never crossed your mind to write prose or verse
and so leave behind you traces of yourself.
That was your charm and then my self-disgust.
It was also my fear—that you'd drive me back
into the croaking mire
of the neoteroi.

7

The self-pity, endless pain and anguish
of one who worships this world and hopes without hope
for another…(Who dares to speak of another world!).

"Strange piety…" (Azucena, Act II).

8

Your speech, so sparing and unguarded,
remains the one thing that satisfies me.
But the accent is different, the color changed.
I'll get accustomed to hearing you or deciphering you
in the ticking of the teletype,
in the shifting smoke
                    from my Brissago cigars.

9

Listening was the only way you had of seeing.
Now the phone bill is down to next to nothing.

10

"Did she pray?" "Yes, she prayed to St Anthony
Because he helps to find
lost umbrellas and other things
from St Hermes' closet."
"Only for that?" "Also for her dead
and for me."
            "That's enough," said the priest.

11

To remember your tears (mine numbered twice as many)
isn't to blot out your bursts of laughter.
They were like a deposit on your private
Last Judgment, which unfortunately never came to pass.

12

Spring comes along at a mole's pace.
I won't hear you any more talking of poisonous
antibiotics, the spike in your femur,
the patrimony you were fleeced of
by a predatory nonentity.

Spring approaches with its thick fogs,
longer days, and unbearable hours.
I won't hear you any more struggling
with time, ghosts, or the logistical
problems of summer.

13

Your brother died young; you were
the disheveled girl who looks out at me
"posed" in an oval portrait.
He wrote music, unpublished, unheard,
now buried in a trunk or rotted away.
Perhaps someone's reinventing it
unwittingly, if what's written is written.
I loved him without having known him.
Except for you, no one remembered him.
I made no inquiries; now there's no point.
After you I'm the only one left
for whom he existed. But it's possible,
you know, to love a shade,
being ourselves shades.

They say that mine
is a poetry of not belonging.
But if it was yours it was someone's—
you who are no longer form but essence.
They say that the highest poetry
praises the Oneness of life as it flees,
denying that the tortoise
is quicker than lightning.
Only you knew that motion
is not different from statis,
the void is fullness and a clear sky
the most diffuse of clouds.
So I understand better your long journey
imprisoned in bandages and plasters.
And yet it doesn't comfort me
to know that as one or as two
we are a single thing.

Xenia II
Eugenio Montale

1

Death didn't concern you.
Though among the dead were your two dogs
and the asylum doctor known as the Demented Uncle,
as well as your mother with her "speciality"
of rice and frogs—a Milanese triumph—
and even your father, who evening and morning
watches me from a miniature
portrait on the wall.
Despite all this, death didn't concern you.

It was I who attended the funerals,
unseen in a taxi standing a ways off
to avoid tears and irritations. Not even
life and its exhibitions of vanity and greed
mattered to you, and so
so much less the universal gangrenes
that transform men into wolves.

A tabula rasa; except
that there came a point, incomprehensible to me,
and this point *concerned you.*

2

You were too often reminded (I seldom was) of Herr Cap.
"I saw him on Ischia, on the bus, maybe twice.
He's a lawyer in Klagenfurt, the one who sends his
    best wishes.
He's supposed to come for a visit."

And finally he comes. I tell him everything:
    he's dumbfounded.
It seems it's a catastrophe for him as well. For a while he
    says nothing.
Then he stands up, mumbling and stiff, and assures me
he'll send his best wishes.
                    It's strange
how the most unlikely people turned out to
    understand you.
Counselor Cap. What a name! And Celia. What became
    of her?

3

For a long time the shoehorn was missing,
that rusted tin horn we took with us everywhere,
though to carry so indecorous a thing
among the tombac and stucco seemed indecent.
It must have been at the Danieli that I forgot
to put it back into the suitcase or small bag.
I'm sure that Hedia the chambermaid threw it
into the Grand Canal. And how could I have written
that I was searching for three inches of tin?
Prestige (*ours*) had to be saved
and Hedia, the faithful, had saved it.

4

Uncannily
escaping from the jaws of Etna
or the teeth of ice,
you came out
with incredible revelations.

Mangano, the good surgeon, witnessed one:
you exposed him as the Black Shirts' cudgel,
and he smiled.

That was you: even on the edge of the abyss
sweetness and terror in a single note.

5

I've descended, your arm in mine, almost a million stairs
and now that you're not here a void opens at every step.
Even so, our long journey was brief.
Mine still goes on, though I no longer feel the need
for connections, reservations,
mix-ups, the scorn of those who believe
that reality is what one sees.

I've descended millions of stairs, your arm in mine,
not, of course, because four eyes see better than two.
I descended them with you because I knew
that between us the only true pupils,
however clouded over, were yours.

6

The wine steward poured you a little
Inferno. And you, frightened: "Must I drink it?
Isn't it enough to be there slowly burning?"

7

"I've never been sure of being in the world."
"How clever," you responded. "And me?"
"Oh, you've nibbled at the world's edges,
if only in homeopathic doses. But I..."

8

"And Paradise? Does paradise exist?"
"I believe so, Signora,
but no one drinks sweet wines any more."

9

Nuns and widows, those deadly,
malodorous, professional mourners,
you wouldn't let yourself look at them.
You were sure that even he
who has a thousand eyes
turns away from them.
The all-seeing, him…judicious,
you didn't call him god,
not even with a small g.

10

I'd been looking a long time
when finally I found you in a bar
on the Avenida da Liberdade. You didn't know
a single world of Portuguese—or rather,
knew a single word: Madeira. And a small glass came
along with a plate of shrimp.

That evening they likened me to illustrious
Lusitanians with unpronounceable names
and, to top it off, to Carducci.
I saw you, unimpressed, hidden in a crowd,
laughing so hard you were crying;
bored, perhaps, but with compunction.

11

Resurfacing out of an infinity of time,
Celia the Phillipina called
just to see how you were doing.
"I believe she's well," I said,
"maybe better than before." "What? You believe?"
Isn't she there?" "Maybe more than before, but…
Celia, try to understand…"

On the other end of the line,
in Manila or some other
name on the map, stammering
stymied even her. And she slammed down the phone.

12

The hawks
always too far away for you,
you seldom saw them really well.
The one at Étretat that watched
the clumsy flights of its young.
Two others in Greece, on the road to Delphi,
a scuffle of soft feathers, two beaks,
young, ardent and harmless.

You liked life ripped to shreds,
whatever broke free of its unbearable
form.

13

I have hung up in my room the daguerreotype
of your father as a child: it's more than a century old.
In the absence of my own (a confused thing),
I try to reconstruct, unsuccessfully, your pedigree.
We aren't horses, our ancestors' lines
aren't in the books. Those who presumed
to know such things did not themselves exist,
nor did we for them. And so? It's still the case
that something happened, perhaps a nothing
that is everything.

The flood has covered the clutter of furniture,
papers, and paintings that filled
a basement locked with a double lock.
Perhaps the red moroccos fought blindly,
and so too the endless dedications of Du Bos,
the wax seal with Ezra's beard,
Alain's Valery, the first edition
of *Canti Orfici*—not to mention some shaving
brushes, a thousand trifles, and all
your brother Silvio's music.
Ten, twelve days in the atrocious hold
of naphtha and dung. Surely they suffered
a lot before losing their identity.
I too am encrusted up to the neck,
but my civil status was dubious from the start.
It's not the muck that besieges me, but the events
of a reality that's unbelievable
and never believed in.
In the face of it all, courage
was the first gift you gave me,
and perhaps you didn't know it.

Heroism
Eugenio Montale

Clizia used to suggest that I join
the partisans in Spain, and more than once I saw myself
dead in Guadalajara or an illustrious survivor
barely able to stand after years in the galleys.
But nothing like that ever occurred: fate denied me
even the rally where my torrents of words
were rewarded with fame and future assignments.
But where have I seen action, I, who do not love
the flocking of the inane and refugees?
I remember one thing: a prisoner of mine
who had a Rilke in his pocket and we were friends
for a few moments; and of no moment then
were the labors, thudding shells, and annoying
ticking of snipers.
Or so it seemed—though not to her
who didn't love homelands and had one only by chance.

In the Smoke
Eugenio Montale

How many times I waited for you at the station
in the cold, the fog. I'd stroll up and down,
coughing, buying unspeakable newspapers,
smoking the Giubas later banned by that fool
the Minister of Tobacco.
Sometimes the wrong train, or one added late
or out of service. I'd inspect
the baggage cars, certain that I'd see
your bags and, behind them, you.
Then finally you appeared. It's a memory
among so many others, and it haunts my dreams.

Late at Night
Eugenio Montale

A colloquy with the shades
isn't something for the telephone.
Our mute conversations are carried on
without a portable or loudspeaker.
And yet we attend to words
even when they don't concern us—
picked up by mistake by an operator
and connected to someone
who isn't there,
who doesn't hear.
One time they came from Vancouver
late at night
while I was holding for Milan. I was surprised
at first, then hoped the strange mistake
would go on. One voice from the Pacific,
the other from the lagoon. And that time
the two voices spoke freely as never before.
For a while nothing happened.
We assured the operator that everything
was all right, perfect, and could—
in fact, must—continue. We never knew
who paid the bill for that miracle.
And I don't recall a word of it.
The time zone was different, the other
voice wasn't here, I wasn't there for her,
even the languages were jumbled, a pot-
pourri of jargon, swearing, and laughter.
Now after so many years the other voice
doesn't remember it and maybe believes I'm dead.
I believe she is the dead one.
For a time anyway she was alive
and was never aware of it.

Singing

Primo Levi

…But when we began to sing
Our songs, senseless and good,
It seemed that everything
Stood as it once had stood.

The days were merely days,
And seven made a week.
Killing we thought was wicked.
Of dying we didn't think.

The months sped by so fast,
With too many to come for complaints!
Again we were only young:
Not martyrs, the shamed, or saints.

We had these thoughts and others
For as long as we could sing.
But it's all hard to explain,
Being a cloudlike thing.

January 3, 1946

Sunset at Fossoli
Primo Levi

I know what it means not to return.
Through barbed wire I have seen
The sun go down and die,
And have felt my flesh torn
By an old poet's words:
"The sun may set and rise,
But we, contrariwise,
Sleep after our short light
One everlasting night."

February 7, 1946

Pliny

Primo Levi

Don't hold me back, my friends, but let me sail.
I won't go far—only as far as the other shore.
I want to see up close that mottled cloud
Rising above Vesuvius, and discover
Where it is this strange light's coming from.

Won't you go with me, nephew? Well, stay and study.
Transcribe those notes I left you yesterday.
Don't be afraid of the ash: ash from ashes,
We ourselves are ash: you remember Epicurus?
Quick, prepare the ship. Already night is falling.

Night at midday: a wonder never seen before.
Don't be afraid, sister. I am careful and competent.
The years that have stooped me haven't idly passed.
I'll soon be back. Just give me time enough
To row across, observe these things, and return.

That way I'll have a new chapter tomorrow
For my books, which I hope will live on
When for centuries the atoms of this old body
Have whirled loose in the vortices of the universe,
Or returned as an eagle, a young girl, or a flower.

Sailors, obey me: shove the ship out to sea.

May 23, 1978

The Little Girl of Pompeii
Primo Levi

Because everyone's anguish is our anguish, we
Go on reliving yours, thin little girl

Who held yourself convulsively to your mother
As though you wanted to be inside her again

When in the afternoon the sky turned black.
No use. Because the air becoming poison

Filtered to find you through the closed window
Of your peaceful, solidly built house, already

Made happy by your singing and shy smile.
Centuries have passed, the ash has petrified,

Imprisoning forever your soft limbs.
So you will remain among us, contorted chalk,

Endless agony, terrible testimony
To how little the gods care for our poor seed.

But nothing remains of your faraway sister,
The young Dutch girl walled up within four walls,

Who nevertheless wrote of her futureless youth.
Her mute dust has been scattered by the wind,

Her brief life locked inside a worn-out notebook.
Nothing remains of the Hiroshima schoolgirl,

A wall shadow cast by the light of a thousand suns,
A victim sacrificed on the altar of fear.

You, powerful ones, owners of new poison,
Sad secret keepers of the definitive thunder,

The sky's afflictions are more than enough for us.
Before you push the button, stop and consider.

November 20, 1978

Brown Battalion
Primo Levi

Is it possible to adopt a more absurd route?
In San Martino Street there is an anthill

Half a meter from the streetcar line,
And right there at the base of one of the rails

A long brown battalion of ants is unwinding.
Muzzle to muzzle one ant meets another,

Perhaps to learn news of their journeys or fortune.
In short, these stupid sisters

Nervous obstinate industrious
Have excavated their city inside our city,

Mapped out their line of tracks beside our tracks.
And they run over ours without suspecting,

Indefatigable in their precarious business,
Taking no notice...
                    I don't want to write about it,

I don't want to write about this brown battalion.
I don't want to write about any brown battalion.

August 13, 1980

Wooden Heart
Primo Levi

My next-door neighbor is robust: a horse
Chestnut tree in Re Umberto Street.

It's as old as I am, but doesn't show it.
It takes in sparrows and blackbirds and isn't ashamed.

In April it presses out buds and leaves,
Fragile flowers in May,

And in September husks with harmless thorns
And shiny tannic chestnuts inside the husks.

It's an impostor, but innocent, pretending
To be emulating its good mountain brother,

Lord of sweet fruits and precious mushrooms.
But its life is hard. Every five minutes

Trams No. 18 and 19 trample its roots.
Stunned by that, it grows bent to one side

As though it wanted to get out of here.
Year after year, it sucks in slow poisons

From the subsoil saturated with methane.
It gets its water from urinating dogs.

The wrinkles in its cork skin are chock full
Of the septic dusk swirling in the streets.

Beneath its bark, dead chrysalises hang,
Which never will change into butterflies.

Yet even so, in its tired wooden heart,
It feels and takes joy in the turning seasons.

May 10, 1980

The Snail
Primo Levi

Why hurry at all when you're so well protected?
Why should one place be better than another
As long as you're not without dampness and grass?
Why run, and run the risk of an accident,
When by retreating into yourself you're at peace?
And even if the world proves hostile then,
You seal yourself off from it silently
Behind your veil of clear innocuous chalk,
Denying the world, and denying yourself to it.
But when the meadow is watery with dew
Or rain has rendered the earth mild again,
Every route becomes your thoroughfare,
The paving beautiful shining slimy liquid,
Bridging leaf to leaf and stone to stone.
You navigate with care, secretly, safely,
Testing the way with telescopic eyes,
Graceful, filthy, logarithmic,
Until you find the other female/male,
And anxious, tensed, and pulsing from your shell,
You know the shy charms of ambiguous love.

December 7, 1983

The Thaw
Primo Levi

When the snow has melted entirely,
We will go looking for the old footpath
Now covered by the blackberry bushes
Behind the wall of the monastery.
Then all will be as it was formerly.

On either side, in the thick shrubbery,
We will find again a certain herb
Whose name I could never tell you.
I change it every Friday,
But forget it every Saturday.
I was told it is rare
And good for melancholy.

The ferns along the path's borders
Are as tender as small creatures:
They barely surface from the ground,
Curled in spirals, and yet
They are ready by now for their loves,
Alternate, green, and more intricate than ours.

Their germs are gnawing at what's holding back
The males and females
In the rusty spore-sac.
They will burst out in the first downpour,
Aswim at the first drop,
Yearning and agile. Long live the married pairs!

We're tired of winter now.
Frost has done all that it could
To flesh, mind, mud, and wood.
May the thaw come and melt the memory
Of last year's snow.

February 2, 1985

Notes

Page 11: "Deor" is preserved in the *Exeter Book*, an anthology of Anglo-Saxon poetry that was donated to the Exeter cathedral library, where it still is, in 1071, by Leofric, the first bishop of Exeter. The poem is probably the work of a *scop* of the 9th century. It contains lines of Christian consolation that, feeling them to be at odds with the spirit of the poem, and disliking them, I have omitted. In his translation, published in *The Word Exchange: Anglo-Saxon Poems in Translation* (2010), Seamus Heaney retains the lines.

Page 76 "Singing": cf. Siegfried Sassoon, "Everyone Sang" (Primo Levi's note).

Page 77 "Sunset at Fossoli": cf. Catullus, *Catulli liber*, 5, 4. At Fossoli, near Modena, there was a detention and selection camp for prisoners destined for deportation. (Primo Levi's note).

Lines 6-9 are Walter Ralegh's translation of Catullus' lines.

Page 78 "Pliny": By getting too close to the volcano, Pliny the Elder died in 79 A.D. during the eruption of Vesuvius that destroyed Pompeii. (Primo Levi's note).

The "nephew" in line 6 is Pliny the Younger, who described his uncle's final hours and death in a famous letter to Tacitus.

Page 80 "Brown Battalion": cf. *Purgatorio*, Canto XXVI. 1.34. (Primo Levi's note).

The translations of Primo Levi's poems were done with Marco Sonzogni of New Zealand.